Disney's

My Very First Winni

Pooh's Jingle Bells

To Anna
From Santa
Christmas 1999

Kathleen Weidner Zoehfeld Illustrated by Robbin Cuddy

SCHOLASTIC INC.
New York Toronto London Auckland Sydney
Mexico City New Delhi Hong Kong

ISBN 0-439-11213-3

Based on the Pooh stories by A. A. Milne (copyright The Pooh Properties Trust).

12 11 10 9 8 7 6 5 4 3 2 1   9/9 0 1 2 3 4/0

Printed in the U.S.A.   24

First Scholastic printing, November 1999

Disney's

My Very First Winnie the Pooh

Pooh's Jingle Bells

"Mmmmm, I love Christmas Eve," said Winnie the Pooh, patting his tummy. "Tomorrow my stocking will be full of brand-new honeypots!"

"Presents are fun," agreed Christopher Robin, "but getting presents isn't the most important thing about Christmas, you know."

Pooh scratched behind his ear. "I suppose there *ARE* other things about Christmas," he said, though he couldn't remember any at the moment.

"Christmas is a time for thinking of others and helping," said Christopher Robin.

Pooh thought about Santa delivering presents all over the world. "Nobody needs more help than Santa!" he cried. "If only we had a sleigh, we could help him deliver presents in it!"

"Good thinking," said Christopher Robin. "Let's go see if anyone has a sleigh we can use."

They found Piglet outside his door, sweeping snow and singing:

Jingle bells, jingle bells, jingle all the way!
Oh, what fun it is to ride
in a one-horse open sleigh. . . .

"That's an idea," said Pooh.

"What is?" asked Piglet.

"A one-horse open sleigh," replied Pooh. "That ought to get us to the North Pole."

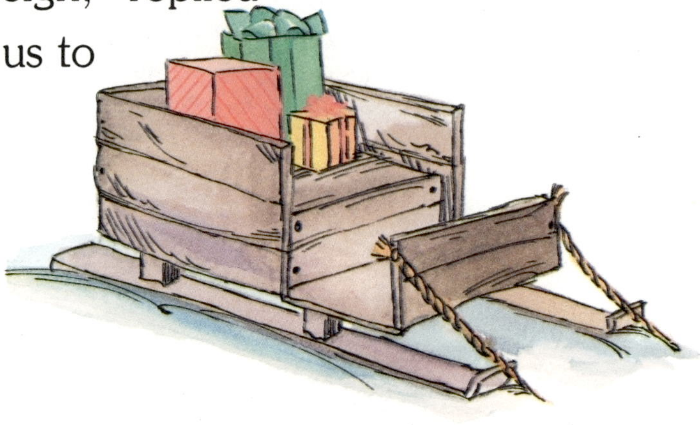

"The N-north Pole!" cried Piglet.

"Yes," said Pooh. "Christopher Robin says Christmas is about helping others, and nobody needs more help than Santa."

"What a grand idea!" cried Piglet. "I'd like to go, too, but I have to finish clearing my walk."

"We can help you with that," said Christopher Robin.

Together they shovelled until the snow was piled up neatly on both sides of Piglet's path.

"Now let's go and see if Kanga knows anything about a sleigh," said Pooh.

They found Roo in his front yard, jingling his jingle bells.

"Oh," cried Piglet, "jingle bells are just what we need for our one-horse open sleigh!"

"A sleigh! A sleigh!" sang Roo. "Where is it?"

"Well, we don't exactly have it yet," explained Pooh. "But when we do, we're going to take it to the North Pole and help Santa deliver presents."

"What a nice idea," said Kanga.

"Do you have a sleigh we can borrow?" asked Christopher Robin.

"No," said Kanga, "but Tigger's coming over soon. I'm sure he'll let you borrow his. Now come in and warm yourselves, while I bake these Christmas cookies."

"Can we help you make them? asked Pooh.

"Certainly, dear," said Kanga.

Together, they sifted flour and spices—then they stirred in butter and honey. And soon, the delicious smell of cookies was coming from Kanga's oven.

"Mmmmmm, yummy!" cried Tigger as he bounced through the front door.

For a while, the cookies made everyone forget all about helping Santa. But Piglet suddenly remembered: "Tigger, we need to borrow your sleigh, so we can help Santa deliver his presents."

"When it comes to helping Santa, Tiggers are the best!" cried Tigger.

Everyone piled onto Tigger's sled. Roo jingled his jingle bells. Everyone sang:

Jingle bells, jingle bells,
jingle all the way!

They swooshed down Kanga's hill toward Rabbit's house.

Dashing through the snow,
In a one-horse open sleigh,
O'er the fields we go,
Laughing all the way. . . .

The wind blew and the snowflakes flew. Everyone laughed and shouted.

"Are we at the North Pole yet?" asked Roo, as the sled scrunched to a stop.

"We've been going DOWN for quite some time," said Pooh thoughtfully, "it seems to me the North Pole must be more UP."

Rabbit, Owl, and Eeyore were gathered in front of Rabbit's house. "The North Pole!" exclaimed Rabbit. "You're not even close."

"Besides," said Eeyore, "it's time to decorate the big pine. Or did you forget?" He held up a long cranberry chain.

RABBIT

"Oh yes!" cried Christopher Robin.

Together they hung candy canes and popcorn balls. Then they stood back and admired their beautiful tree.

Piglet nudged Pooh. "What about Santa?"

"Oh!" cried Pooh. "We've got to get to the North Pole to help Santa before it's too late!"

"And you plan to reach the North Pole in this?" asked Owl, pointing to Tigger's sled.

"Yes," said Pooh.

"Well then, you'll need some locomotion," said Owl.

"A loco-what?" asked Pooh.

"*A horse*, perhaps," said Owl.

"Oh," said Pooh. "We forgot that part!"

Everyone looked at Eeyore.

"Don't look at me," said Eeyore.

"You'd be a great horse!" cried Christopher Robin.

"It's a simple matter of attaching him to the sleigh correctly," said Rabbit. He tied Eeyore to the sled with ropes.

"Not too tight around the middle," sighed Eeyore.

"The perfect one-horse open sleigh!" exclaimed Owl, admiring Rabbit's work.

Roo jingled his jingle bells.
Eeyore puffed and pulled.
Everyone sang:

Bells on bobtail ring,
Making spirits bright,
What fun it is to ride and sing
A sleighing song tonight!

Eeyore had trotted happily quite some distance when Christopher Robin noticed that the sun was sinking low in the sky. "I've been thinking," he said. "If we go all the way to the North Pole, we might not have time to give our presents to each other."

"Oh no!" cried Pooh. "Maybe GETTING presents is not the most important thing about Christmas, but GIVING is important."

"Oh d-dear," said Piglet, "I'm sure Santa wouldn't want us to forget that!"

"Keep singing that nice jingly tune," said Eeyore, "and I'll have us around the Hundred-Acre Wood in no time."

Together they laughed and sang and jingled their way from house to house, delivering presents to all their friends.

"We're helping Santa! We're helping Santa!" sang Roo.

"So we are," said Pooh. "We're Santa's helpers after all!"